TRAILBLAZING FEMALE ATHLETES

TRAILBLAZING WOMEN IN
TENNIS

BY MATT DOEDEN

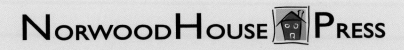

NORWOOD HOUSE PRESS

Cover: Naomi Osaka played at the US Open in 2021.

Norwood House Press

For information regarding Norwood House Press, please visit our website at:
www.norwoodhousepress.com or call 866-565-2900.

Credits
Editor: Katharine Hale
Designer: Becky Daum
Fact Checker: Lillian Dondero

PHOTO CREDITS: Cover: © Garrett Ellwood/USTA/AP Images; © AP Images, 5, 9, 13, 16, 19, 21; © Lev Radin/Shutterstock Images, 7, 35, 41, 45; © Leonard Zhukovsky/Shutterstock Images, 11, 29, 34, 39; © Kathy Hutchins/Shutterstock Images, 22, 31; © Richard Sheinwald/AP Images, 24; © Robert Dear/AP Images, 25, 27; © Jamie Squire/Allsport/Getty Images Sport/Getty Images, 33; © Dana Gardner/Shutterstock Images, 36; © Frank Franklin II/AP Images, 43

Library of Congress Cataloging-in-Publication Data
Names: Doeden, Matt, author.
Title: Trailblazing women in tennis / by Matt Doeden.
Description: Chicago: Norwood House Press, 2023. | Series: Trailblazing female athletes | Includes bibliographical
    references and index. | Audience: Grades 4-6
Identifiers: LCCN 2022005093 (print) | LCCN 2022005094 (ebook) | ISBN 9781684507528 (hardcover) | ISBN
    9781684048038 (paperback) | ISBN 9781684048090 (ebook)
Subjects: LCSH: Women tennis players--Biography--Juvenile literature.
Classification: LCC GV994.A1 D64 2023 (print) | LCC GV994.A1 (ebook) |DDC 796.342082--dc23/eng/20220209
LC record available at https://lccn.loc.gov/2022005093
LC ebook record available at https://lccn.loc.gov/2022005094

Hardcover ISBN: 978-1-68450-752-8
Paperback ISBN: 978-1-68404-803-8

353N—082022
Manufactured in the United States of America in North Mankato, Minnesota.

CONTENTS

HISTORY OF TENNIS

Women's tennis is one of the most popular sports in the world. Fans love its high-speed serves, dramatic **volleys**, and engaging superstars. It's an action-packed game filled with thrilling rivalries. Emotional wins and devastating defeats thrill fans worldwide. There's a constant battle for the title of the world's best player.

It hasn't always been that way, though. In the early days of women's tennis, players who earned money from tennis could not compete in tournaments. People of color rarely competed. The sport didn't fill arenas. It didn't get major TV deals. Tennis stars got little fanfare.

That began to change in 1968. New rules allowed **professional** players to enter tournaments. That meant players could

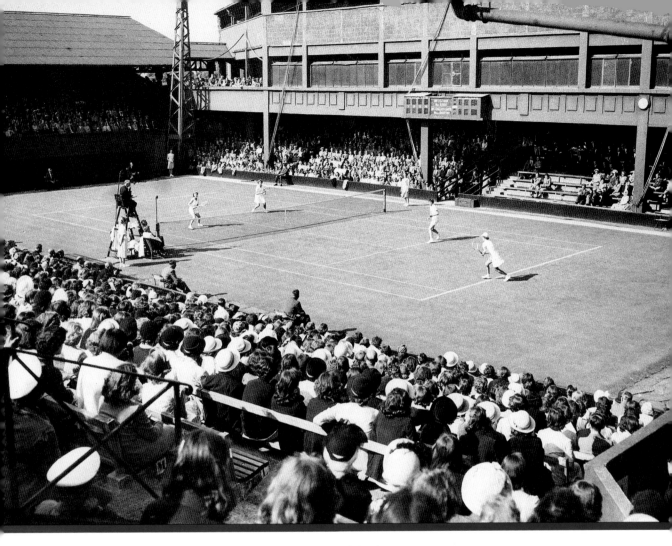

Before 1968, tournaments such as Wimbledon were not open to professional tennis players.

finally make a living by playing tennis. It was the start of what's called the Open Era.

The modern game barely resembles tennis from before the Open Era. Today's players are worldwide celebrities.

They come from a wide range of ethnic backgrounds. The best players make millions of dollars each year in winnings and **endorsements**.

Those changes didn't just happen. From tennis's earliest stars to modern superstars, the players worked to make the game more inclusive. This includes embracing players for who they are. They have made the game into a booming business, with many players earning huge paydays. And they've used their fame to support causes that matter to them.

Over the decades, countless players have done their part. But a handful have helped advance the sport in groundbreaking ways. Suzanne Lenglen became tennis's first superstar in the early 1900s. Billie Jean King fought for **equality** on and off the court. Martina Navratilova changed the way the game was played. Serena Williams became a global icon. Naomi Osaka broke down cultural barriers on her way to the top. These are only some of the players who have blazed the trail to make tennis what it is today.

(From left) Naomi Osaka, Billie Jean King, and Serena Williams are some of the biggest trailblazers in tennis history. They inspire future generations of tennis players.

CHAPTER ONE

SUZANNE LENGLEN

Women's tennis was growing in popularity in the early 1900s. Wimbledon is the sport's most famous tournament. Women had played there since 1884. They had competed in the Olympics since 1900. Yet the sport got little press coverage. It struggled to attract fans. Tennis was missing a key element to capturing the public's attention. It needed a superstar.

Suzanne Lenglen was born on May 24, 1899, in Paris, France. From an early age, she was an excellent athlete. Lenglen started playing tennis at the age of 11. Her father, Charles, gave her a child's racket and some old tennis balls. Just a month after she started playing, she won her first **amateur** tournament. Her father saw her talent. He pushed her to practice and become the best tennis player she could be. Her training

Suzanne Lenglen made headlines for her impressive tennis game as well as her unconventional clothing.

was difficult. Charles pushed Suzanne hard. She often ended practice in tears.

Breaking Out

Lenglen made her mark in 1914. She and partner Max Decugis won the mixed doubles title at the French Championships.

Then Lenglen won the World Hard Court Championships in Paris. It was Lenglen's first major singles title. She was just 15 years old.

Lenglen's career was just taking off. But then World War I (1914–1918) started. The war brought most sports to a halt. Lenglen lost some of the prime years of her career to the conflict.

Back on the Court

In 1919, Lenglen headed to Great Britain to compete at Wimbledon. Lenglen advanced to the finals. She faced the defending champion, Dorothea Lambert Chambers. It was a hard-fought, back-and-forth match. More than 8,000 people watched. Lenglen won. She became the first non-British woman to claim the trophy.

Lenglen's 1919 Wimbledon victory marked the start of her best years. She was a force on the court. Over the next

The French Open is played at Roland-Garros in Paris. A memorial to Suzanne Lenglen stands outside a court named for her there.

seven years, Lenglen lost only one singles match. She won the Wimbledon title five years in a row from 1919 to 1923. She won again in 1925. There was no denying that she was the biggest star in women's tennis.

But Lenglen didn't dominate only in singles.

QUICK FACT

Suzanne Lenglen's nickname was "The Goddess." The French media often called her "Our Suzanne."

She also played doubles with American player Elizabeth Ryan. They would go on to become one of the most successful doubles teams in tennis history. The pair won doubles at Wimbledon six times between 1919 and 1925.

Blazing a Trail

Lenglen's skill on the court led to great success. Her personality helped make her a major star. At the time, women were expected to play tennis in dresses. The long clothing covered their arms and their legs. It wasn't suited for quick, fluid movement. Lenglen rejected the traditional clothing. She brought her own sense of practical style to the court. Lenglen wasn't afraid to be loud or brash. She went against ideas of

The Match of the Century

Suzanne Lenglen and American Helen Wills were the two biggest women's tennis stars of the 1920s. Yet they faced each other only one time, in 1926. It was called the Match of the Century. More than 6,000 people came to watch the clash. Lenglen won both sets to stake her claim as the greatest of her generation.

Suzanne Lenglen (left) played American Helen Wills in 1926.

how women should behave. Many fans loved her for it. Others thought she should behave more like the other players.

In 1926, Lenglen took another big step that would change her career. At the time, tennis was considered an amateur sport. Players who earned money from the game couldn't compete in tournaments. Professional players did tennis tours instead. Lenglen headlined a tennis tour in the United States. She was the star of the show. She earned more money in 1927 than baseball star Babe Ruth. But touring meant Lenglen could no longer compete in the game's biggest tournaments. Wimbledon took away her membership. The French tennis association banned her. Lenglen spoke out against the amateur model. She said it was unfair to the players. They could not earn money from the sport. This meant only wealthy people could compete.

Lenglen remained active in the game. She became a tennis teacher. But her health declined in the 1930s. She died on July 4, 1938. She was only 39 years old.

Style Matters

Suzanne Lenglen became almost as famous for her fashion as for her tennis game. She came to matches dressed in full-length fur coats and heavy makeup. She wore her hair in a short style called a bob. Even on the court she set trends. She played in clothing that exposed her arms and lower legs. Women in her time were expected to remain covered. Her bold outfits sparked controversy.

CHAPTER TWO

BILLIE JEAN KING

Billie Jean Moffitt was born on November 22, 1943, in Long Beach, California. Both of her parents had been active in sports. Her brother Randy became a baseball star. Moffitt dreamed of being a professional athlete, too. But in the 1950s, there were few opportunities for women to make a living in sports. She started out playing basketball and softball. But she switched to tennis around age 11.

Even at a young age, Moffitt was a powerful player. She played an **aggressive** style. This was not common at the time in the women's game. But Moffitt was not afraid to go against what was normal. For instance, during the 1950s, women traditionally wore dresses while playing. Moffitt preferred shorts.

Billie Jean King was a top tennis player in the 1960s, 1970s, and early 1980s.

Rising Star

At age 15, Moffitt began playing in major tournaments. She quickly started climbing up the world rankings. In 1961, she made headlines at Wimbledon. She and her partner, Karen Hantze Susman, won the doubles title. Moffitt was just 17.

Susman was 18. That made them the youngest team to win the title.

Even with her success, Moffitt couldn't earn a living playing tennis. Tennis rules barred her from earning money from the sport. She worked other jobs to make ends meet.

In 1965, Moffitt married Larry King. He was a law student and college tennis player. She took his last name, becoming Billie Jean King. She began to focus more on her tennis

career. It paid off. She won her first **Grand Slam** singles title at Wimbledon in 1966. She defended that title in 1967 and 1968. She had success in other tournaments as well. King was becoming a tennis superstar. She went on to win 12 Grand Slam singles titles. She also won 27 Grand Slam doubles and mixed doubles titles with various partners. This made her one of the greatest players of her generation.

Winning the Battle

King was enjoying huge success on the court. And the dawn of the Open Era allowed her to make a living off her skills. Yet the women's game still didn't get the press coverage of the men's game. Bobby Riggs was a former men's tennis champion. He bragged that even at age 55, he could beat the top-rated women. Riggs challenged King to prove him wrong.

The Big Screen

In 2017, Fox Searchlight Pictures released a feature film called *Battle of the Sexes*. The film centered on Billie Jean King, Bobby Riggs, and their famous match. Actress Emma Stone played the part of King. She was nominated for a Golden Globe Award for Best Actress.

The Battle of the Sexes was a prime-time spectacle. King was carried onto the court before the match.

At first, King declined. She didn't need to prove herself to a man who didn't respect women. But Riggs made her an offer she couldn't refuse. The Battle of the Sexes would be a winner-take-all match for $100,000. This would be worth more than $600,000 in 2022. King knew a win would show people that women's tennis should be taken seriously. The match was set for September 20, 1973.

It was an event made for television. King and Riggs played up their rivalry. Riggs lobbed sexist comments at King. She got Riggs back by gifting him a live pig. The two built up publicity for their event. The Battle of the Sexes was big news. Fans couldn't wait to see if Riggs could back up his bragging. But it wasn't much of a contest. Riggs hadn't focused on training. He underestimated King. King was 26 years younger than Riggs. She was faster, stronger, and in better shape. She won all three sets to claim the title and the prize money.

Push for Equality

King's victory over Riggs helped bring more awareness to women's tennis. She continued to be a force on the court. But she also worked behind the scenes. One example was the US Open. It offered more prize money to men than women. In 1973, King said she would refuse to play in the US Open unless the prize money was equal. Her tactic worked. The US Open became the first Grand Slam tournament to offer equal prize money.

That year, King and her husband helped form the Women's Tennis Association (WTA). The WTA would host a new women's tennis tour. It would fight for greater equality between the men's and women's games. A year later, King was named the WTA's first president.

Billie Jean King holds her trophy after winning the singles title at Wimbledon in 1975.

In 1981, King's career changed forever. A former girlfriend outed King as being gay. King's lawyers denied it. But King refused to lie about who she was. She officially came out as gay. At that time, pro sports had few openly gay athletes. Many of

King's sponsors dropped her. But King's fellow athletes were supportive. WTA president Chris Evert and fellow player Martina Navratilova were outspoken in their support. King was outed before she was ready. But her advocacy helped pave the way for others who followed. Billie Jean and Larry King divorced on friendly terms in 1987.

Billie Jean King began playing doubles with Ilana Kloss (left) in 1982. The two began dating in 1987 and married in 2018.

King officially retired from competition in 1984. But she continued to play. King has remained a major figure in the fight for equality in all women's sports. Her skill on the tennis court and her work for equality off it made her one of the most influential athletes of her generation.

CHAPTER THREE

MARTINA NAVRATILOVA

Martina Navratilova was born on October 18, 1956, in Prague, Czechoslovakia. This is now the Czech Republic. Her grandmother, Agnes Semanska, had been a tennis star. Navratilova's mother played tennis and was also a gymnast. And her stepfather was a tennis teacher. By age four, Navratilova was already banging tennis balls off walls. She was just eight years old when she entered her first tournament. She made it all the way to the semifinals.

Early Career

By 1972, 15-year-old Navratilova was a star on the rise. That year she won the

Martina Navratilova came to the United States in the 1970s to play professional tennis.

Czechoslovakia national championship. She won her first professional tournament in the United States two years later.

Life in the United States was a big change for Navratilova. In Czechoslovakia, the government was very controlling of its citizens. She had to ask the government for permission to compete in tournaments. The freedoms in the United States appealed to the outspoken young star. She wanted to stay and become a US citizen. In 1975, she officially gave up her Czech citizenship. She was ready to play full time against the world's best on her own terms.

Much of Navratilova's early success came in doubles. She teamed up with Chris Evert to win the 1975 French Open. It was Navratilova's first major title. The pair went on to win the Wimbledon doubles title in 1976.

Chris Evert (left) and Martina Navratilova made a strong doubles team and were fierce singles rivals.

Navratilova and Evert were back on the court together at Wimbledon in 1978. But this time they were opponents in the singles final. Evert was the number-one player in the world. But Navratilova put up a tough match. It all came down to the third set.

Navratilova outlasted her friend and rival. She won the set 9–7. It was her first singles title. It marked the beginning of a long run as the world's top player.

The 1980s

Navratilova won 15 Grand Slam singles titles during the 1980s. No woman won more. That included six straight Wimbledon titles. But she made news for more than her game.

In 1981, an article in the New York *Daily News* outed Navratilova as bisexual. She had planned to make the news public. But the article took away her chance to do it on her own terms. It was only a few months after King had been

Chris Evert

Chris Evert was a big part of Martina Navratilova's life and career. Evert, born in 1954, was one of Navratilova's role models. They became friends, playing partners, and eventually the sport's biggest rivals. Evert won 18 Grand Slam singles titles in her career. She also added three doubles titles. Two of them were with Navratilova as her partner. She retired in 1989.

Martina Navratilova holds up her Wimbledon trophy in 1987.

outed. Like King, Navratilova lost some sponsors. But her fellow players were largely supportive. She forged ahead as an advocate for equality in tennis.

Late Career

In 1990, Navratilova won her record ninth Wimbledon title. It would be the final Grand Slam singles title of her career. She reached the Wimbledon final again four years later. But she lost to Conchita Martínez. Still, it was an amazing accomplishment for 37-year-old Navratilova. Most of the sport's star players at the time were in their teens and early twenties.

Speaking Out

Martina Navratilova has used her fame to promote a wide variety of causes. She was a leader in the push for LGBT rights. In 1993, she was a speaker at the March on Washington for Lesbian, Gay, and Bi-Equal Rights and Liberation. She has also spoken out on human rights and animal rights.

Navratilova retired from playing tennis full time in late 1994. But she didn't stop playing completely. She continued entering select events for more than a decade. She even won a Wimbledon match in 2004 at the age of 47. This made her the oldest player ever to win a Grand Slam singles match. Two years later, she played mixed doubles at the US Open. She won her final major title at 49 years old.

Martina Navratilova continued playing well into the 2010s.

CHAPTER FOUR

SERENA WILLIAMS

Serena Williams was born on September 26, 1981. Her father believed she and her older sister Venus could become tennis stars. By age three, Serena was on the court, practicing and mastering her skills.

The Williams family devoted itself to the girls' careers. When Serena was nine years old, the family moved from California to Florida. That way the girls could work with elite coaches. It wasn't always easy for the Williams family. Tennis was a sport dominated by white players. The girls faced racism. But they never stopped working on their dream of becoming the best tennis players in the world.

Venus is 14 months older than Serena. She turned pro in 1994, at the age of 14. Serena

Serena (left) and Venus Williams attend the premiere of *King Richard*. The 2021 film tells the story of the sisters' rise to tennis greatness.

stayed in the amateur ranks. She cheered on her sister. Serena knew that her turn was coming.

Going Pro

Serena Williams played her first professional event in 1995. But her pro career took off in 1997. She made a name for herself at the Ameritech Cup in Chicago, Illinois. Williams entered the tournament ranked 304th in the world.

Few expected much from such a low-ranked player. But Williams surprised everyone. She beat two of the world's top-ten-ranked players before losing in the semifinals. She overwhelmed opponents with her powerful **ground strokes**. Williams quickly rose up the WTA rankings. She won her first singles title in 1999. A few months later, she beat Martina Hingis to win the US Open. Hingis was the world's number-one player. It was Williams's first Grand Slam title.

Venus Williams

Since she turned pro in 1994, Venus Williams has helped change the game. Like her younger sister, Venus thrills fans with her power and speed. She broke out in 2000 when she won both Wimbledon and the US Open. She went on to win seven Grand Slam titles. The last came at Wimbledon in 2008. Venus is also an **activist** for causes such as gender and racial equality.

Serena Williams kisses her trophy after winning her first US Open title.

Williams was becoming almost unstoppable. From 2002 to 2003, she won four straight Grand Slam events. The media nicknamed it a "Serena Slam," meaning that she held all four titles at once.

The Rio 2016 Olympics were Serena Williams's fourth appearance at the Games.

Total Domination

For more than a decade, Williams dominated tennis. She won the Olympic gold medal in singles in 2012. She won a second Serena Slam in 2013 to 2014. From 2013 to 2016, she held the world's number-one ranking for 186 consecutive weeks.

Tennis players traditionally begin to decline in their thirties. But Williams was playing as few before her had ever done.

At the same time, Williams was becoming a fashion and pop culture icon. She earned fame for wearing daring outfits, even during matches. She created two fashion lines, Aneres and S by Serena. She designed handbags, designer nails, and more.

Serena Williams walks the runway for one of her fashion lines.

Williams was also building a family. Entrepreneur Alexis Ohanian proposed to Williams in late 2016. The following January, she won the Australian Open. It was her twenty-third Grand Slam singles title. It was an Open

Serena Williams's catsuit is more than a fashion statement. It can help prevent blood clots, which were a serious concern for the athlete after complications following her pregnancy.

Era record among both women and men. And she'd done it while she was eight weeks pregnant with the couple's first child. Later that year, Williams gave birth to a baby girl. It was a difficult time. Williams nearly died after giving birth. But she fought to return to the court. She continued to compete at the highest levels. Williams breaks race and gender barriers. She has paved the way for future trailblazers.

Althea Gibson

Few players have traveled a tougher road to stardom than Althea Gibson. Born in 1927, Gibson grew up in South Carolina. Jim Crow laws denied black people equal rights. But Gibson was a gifted athlete. She broke through the color barrier to win five Grand Slam singles titles. After her tennis career was over, Gibson switched to professional golf. She fought through racism to help change the way people thought about who could compete at the highest levels.

CHAPTER FIVE

NAOMI OSAKA

Naomi Osaka was born on October 16, 1997, in Osaka, Japan. Her mother, Tamaki, was from Japan. Her father, Leonard, was from Haiti. Growing up in Japan wasn't always easy. Naomi came from an interracial marriage. Many people in Japan did not approve. This included some of Tamaki's family.

In 1999, Leonard watched Venus and Serena Williams play in a tennis tournament. They inspired him. He wanted Naomi and her sister Mari to be like the talented sisters. He started training them. The Williams sisters were among Naomi's tennis heroes, especially Serena. She loved Serena's hard-hitting game. Naomi dreamed of being like her. When Naomi was three years old, the family moved to the United States. They wanted to have better access to courts for training.

Naomi Osaka came to the United States as a child with dreams of becoming a tennis star.

Breaking Out

Naomi and Mari practiced hard. Leonard studied how the Williams family had raised Venus and Serena. He copied a lot of what they had done. That included focusing on practice instead of playing in junior-level competitions.

In 2011, Naomi Osaka started playing at International Tennis Federation (ITF) events. She was 14. In these amateur tournaments, she played against women much older than her. Osaka used her strong serve to hold her own. In 2013, she turned pro. Her first event was the Bank of the West Classic in Stanford, California. She faced Samantha Stosur, a former US Open champion, in her first match.

Osaka lost the first set. But she fought back to take the match. It was a thrilling start to her pro career. She began to climb the WTA rankings. By 2016, she was ranked in the top 50. That year, she was named the WTA Newcomer of the Year.

Climbing to the Top

In 2018, Osaka won her first pro tournament. She beat top-ranked Simona Halep in the semifinals. Osaka went on

Naomi Osaka won her first Grand Slam title in 2018 at the US Open.

to earn the trophy. It was the start of an amazing year. Osaka beat her childhood idol, Serena Williams, in the US Open final. That gave Osaka her first Grand Slam title. Osaka's victory marked the first time a Japanese player had won a Grand Slam singles title. She had another Grand Slam win at the

2019 Australian Open. That made her the world's new number-one player. It was a dream come true.

Osaka continued to dominate women's tennis. She also used her fame to speak out for causes important to her. One of those causes was racial justice. In the 2020 US Open, she wore face masks with the names of Black Americans who had been killed

Emotional Match

The 2018 final between Naomi Osaka and Serena Williams was full of drama and emotion. Osaka controlled the match with powerful volleys. Frustrated, Williams slammed her racket down. An official gave Williams a penalty. The crowd booed the official. They kept booing when Osaka went on to win. Osaka was in tears. She didn't feel as if she could celebrate one of the biggest moments of her career. But Williams joined her on the court after the match. She put her arm around Osaka in support. They celebrated Osaka's first Grand Slam victory together.

Naomi Osaka uses her platform to promote racial justice and mental health.

by police and racial violence. Another important cause was mental health. Osaka opened up about her own mental health struggles. She pulled herself out of the 2021 French Open.

She said the pressure from reporters was too much. Many fellow athletes and sponsors hurried to support her.

Osaka remained one of the game's best players. Her high-speed serves and powerful ground strokes made her a force on the court. Her image, personality, and off-the-court life made her a fan favorite. She became one of the most influential athletes in the world. In 2021, Osaka became the highest-paid female athlete in history. She made more than $55 million over a 12-month period.

Representing Japan

Naomi Osaka lives in the United States. But she represents Japan in international events. That included the Olympic Games in Tokyo, Japan. They took place in 2021. Osaka lit the Olympic cauldron at the opening ceremony. It was a huge honor. Osaka advanced to the third round of the Olympic tournament. She lost to Markéta Vondroušová of the Czech Republic.

Martina Navratilova (left) and Chris Evert (right) celebrate Serena Williams's 2014 US Open victory.

Tennis has come a long way since its early days. The game's stars have constantly pushed for better pay and equality for all. It's a fight that continues into the modern day. Stars of today and the future will continue to blaze a trail for the players who will follow.

GLOSSARY

activist
a person who promotes causes for social or political change

aggressive
an attacking, high-risk style

amateur
an athlete who is not paid to compete in a sport

endorsements
agreements in which a person is paid to promote a product

equality
equal treatment regardless of race, gender, or sexual orientation

Grand Slam
a term that describes the four biggest tournaments on the tennis tour: the Australian Open, the French Open, Wimbledon, and the US Open; can also refer to the achievement of winning all four tournaments in a year

ground strokes
tennis shots made by hitting a ball that has bounced off the ground

LGBT
an acronym for lesbian, gay, bisexual, and transgender

professional
an athlete who is paid to compete in a sport

volleys
tennis shots made by hitting a ball before it has touched the ground

FOR MORE INFORMATION

Books

London, Martha. *Legends of Women's Tennis*. Mendota Heights, MN: Press Box Books, 2021.

Scheff, Matt. *Naomi Osaka: Tennis Star*. Lake Elmo, MN: Focus Readers, 2020.

Weintraub, Aileen. *We Got Game!: 35 Female Athletes Who Changed the World*. Philadelphia, PA: Running Press Kids, 2020.

Websites

About Naomi Osaka
(www.naomiosaka.com/about)

Naomi Osaka's website introduces visitors to the athlete through videos, photos, and text.

DK FindOut: Tennis
(www.dkfindout.com/us/sports/tennis)

This website gives readers an overview of tennis.

Sports Illustrated Kids: The Debate over Equal Pay in Tennis, Explained
(www.sikids.com/tennis/equal-pay-raymond-moore-billie-jean-king-venus-williams-novak-djokovic-andy-murray)

This article discusses the history of the equal pay debate and how it continues today.

INDEX

ABOUT THE AUTHOR

Matt Doeden began his career as a sportswriter, covering everything from high school sports to the National Football League. Since then, he has written hundreds of children's and young adult books on topics ranging from history to sports to current events. Doeden lives in Minnesota with his wife and two children.